# GRIM FALLACIES

90% of traders fail

How to be in the 10%

Michael Wells

No portion of this book may be reproduced in any form without written permission from the publisher or author, except as permitted by U.S. copyright law.

The author does not make any guarantee as to any results that may be obtained from using the content of this book. You should never make any investment decision without first conducting your own research and due diligence. To the maximum extent permitted by law, the author disclaims any and all liability in the event any information, commentary, analysis, opinions, advice and/or recommendations contained in this book prove to be inaccurate, incomplete or unreliable, or result in any investment or other losses.
Content in this book does not constitute legal advice or investment advice and no attorney-client relationship is formed. The author is providing this book and its contents on an "as is" basis. Your use of the information in this book is at your own risk.

# Table of contents

# Introduction

Since the 2008 financial crisis, people are getting desperate. The world is still not the same as it was before the crisis. There is a major pension problem all over the world and simply leaving money in the bank has become very unprofitable, although less risky and definitely more appealing to the more risk averse people following the events of the 2008 crisis. While households have less debt on average, the global debt continues to grow and people are looking for new and faster ways of making money in this changing economy.

We all know a person who already lost some money with trading, and thinks the markets are just a big casino. I typically ask them this question, If it is all a big casino, how is it possible that so many people are making an incredible living with just trading? Trading has gotten a bad reputation over the recent years and it has become readily available to anyone with a phone. All you need is a trading account and some money, that most people can just charge to their credit card. With huge amounts of leverage freely available, one doesn't even need the necessary capital to take huge positions that could potentially double someone's savings or wipe them out in an instant. It is very easy to lose money in the markets, because people that know how to make money will not hesitate to take it from you if you give them the chance. But it is just as easy to prevent losing money in the market. This should be the main focus and the first thing a new trader learns: To minimize losses. If there was a method to never risk more than 1% of your capital within the trading account it would take 100 losses in a row to wipe an account, and ways like this do exist. So why do so many new traders open up an account, and "blow up" within 3 months?

The general market, as of 2020 has been trending up for the last three decades as shown by indexes like the SPX or the Dow Jones, yet people manage to lose money or have the perception that the markets are a perpetual up and down constantly on the risk of going to zero. Even during the massive crisis of 2008, the markets fell by about 50%, definitely not going to zero, and then rose 50% again after only about 3 months following the crash. After just one year, the values were back to 80% of the value before the crash, and kept steadily rising. The truth is that a good amount of these participants in the markets that lost everything were heavily leveraged, in which case any drop in price could theoretically wipe their entire account, depending on the amount of leverage. Adding to that, there was obviously a great deal of panic selling, further pushing the price down at just the absolute worst levels, and then buying again after the price bounced back up, again at the worst possible levels. A mistake caused by a strong emotional response that even the most trained institutional traders are prone to.

The markets offer an incredible opportunity that has never been so readily available to everyone with just access to the internet, and it ought to be taken advantage of. It can be a powerful tool to deal with the problems of the pension crisis and guarantee a good or even early retirement. It can greatly enhance the quality of life by adding a good amount of extra spending power. It can even change someone's life by creating a whole new career opportunity with more free time and self employment.

But given that most retail traders fail, it is important to understand who the money is being lost to and why. The problem is a major conflict of interest between the naive retail trader, who just got into the business and believes every charlatan trading educator with an IB contract and the various experts on the other side. They know the mindset of the retail trader and their typical mistakes hoping to make money, and they are definitely not just going to give it to you. You would be surprised how many new traders fall for the exact fallacies over and over again.

# Chapter 1: The conflict of interest

*Trading educators*

Trading educators like to form a narrative and make you believe it. They say what the retail traders want to hear. Everyone can do it. You don't need capital or hard work, and you don't need to study. All you need to do is buy their program and follow a pattern on a chart. But there is a very simple reason why the retail trader cannot trust a trading educator: a massive conflict of interest. When stumbling across a trading educator, there are two ways for them to make money. The first one is the program that is supposed to make you rich. They promise a program that will teach you their unique black box trading strategy that can turn X amount of money into a tenfold return every week. The second way is as an Introducing Broker. Every time someone even mentions a broker under the pretence that they are giving you free tips on the internet, they have an IB contract. It is illegal for them to talk about their broker without this contract being in place. If they did, they would be forced to either obtain an IB contract or seize using the brokerage platform that they mentioned. This is a major conflict of interest between you and the trading educator. Their interest lies in trading fees and commission payments every time you place a trade. They want you to trade with them as often as possible. The job of a trading educator with an IB contract is to drive you to their specific broker to earn a commission. Because of that they overstate the importance of the broker and lure the retail trader onto the platform with promises of fancy charting tools and analytical software that you allegedly need.

The plain truth is, that a broker is just an execution tool for the successful trader. All you need is two buttons: Buy and sell. Everything else that they try to sell as the magic solution that will make you into a professional trader is just marketing that institutional traders laugh at. They are not going through brokers unlike the retail trader anyway. They don't have to since they have direct market access. To sum up, anyone who shows their broker while giving trading advice has a major conflict of interest, and a professional trader would most likely not trust a single word they say.

Trading educators like to brand themselves with very specific titles. They are „crypto swing traders" or „forex day traders", titles that seem to only benefit the broker anyway as they are conveniently characteristics that brokers love. "Day trader" means that you guarantee the broker at least two payments per day, when opening and closing a position. This is obviously a completely unrealistic and frankly ridiculous thing to say if you are trying to make money. Every asset class and time frame suffers from periods of „bad luck". The saying goes „bad things happen in threes" and that is true for 8 observations as it is 0.5 multiplied by itself three times equals 1/8. If we follow that calculation we conclude that every 64 observations you suffer from bad luck 6 times in a row on average. An observation can be an individual trade however long that may take or one calendar day of the year. So restricting yourself to swing trading, when the market is currently in a period of an uptrend would stop you from making any profit from your system during that period of „bad luck". Why would someone restrict themselves to one asset class or time frame anyway? The same problem goes for time frames. Following a financial crisis or major political event like an election, the market volatility usually goes up significantly allowing for short term trades. During the summer we usually have periods of very low volatility for weeks making day trading impossible. Because the retail trader restricts himself to one time frame, he falls into confirmation bias and constantly loses money on commission fees alone to open and close positions every single day before he realizes that there is no point; the volatility just is not enough. A successful trader distances himself from confirmation bias and emotions during trading as much as possible. He does not day trade because he feels like it on a given day, or because he believes that it is his field of expertise. A successful trader will go with the market and the opportunity and always be open towards the possibility that the markets can change rapidly and require a different strategy.

The reason that retail traders are very easy prey to the trading educator is that they are not only easily influenced, but are actively looking for the meaningless promises that educators make. Everyone has heard of the financial markets and their ability to expose you to huge risk and potentially reward. However risk management and how to put in a trade are not common knowledge, so the average

person goes on the internet and types in „how to trade",
„how to become a trader" or „how to buy stock". The very
first results are always trading educators or even brokers
themselves who paid for the exposure and search result
listing. As the months go by their listing is still up, so one
can draw the conclusion that they made so much money
from posting the advertisement, that they are willing to do
it again. This shows how many people never get past the
first results, and fall into the trap in which they never learn
risk management. In fact it will be shunned.

Due to the conflict of interest the trading educator will
promote all the behaviors comparable to gambling, that
will make them and the broker money with no regard for
your potential losses. But how do they persuade
unsuspecting people into this trap? How do they carefully
craft this relatable, trustworthy persona? The trading
educator successfully forms a false portrayal of their life
consisting of expensive cars, houses and luxury. They show
their successful trades and how much money they made
on that day, always in cash not in percent, by posting a
picture of a chart on a laptop with stacks of cash next to it,
set in front of a beautiful view in a nice house. How could

they fake all of this if they actually have no idea how to trade? The stacks of money are fake and the car/ house are rented for a day. Sometimes they mess up and accidentally show the license plate number which can be looked up to prove that the car was just rented for the day.

The successful trades they show took place but they never made a profit or had any risk in them. They simply open two trading accounts and go long in one account and short the same security in the other account. Then they just post the position that went the right way. Additionally they are deceptive by only showing the cash amount they made and not the amount in percent increase of their total capital. A profit of 1000$ would mean completely doubling your account in one day if the money a person has in the account is only 1000$, which is almost always completely impossible, and definitely impossible in the long term. If the account was 10,000$ and the position with leverage 100,000$, then the profit would be only a single percent, which is an unimpressive return. Since they are hedging by taking the exact position size in both directions between two accounts they have almost zero risk and can take as much leverage as they want to achieve alleged high returns, when in reality they lost the same amount of money in the other account, that they made in the account that they show on their social media. This is how trading educators on the internet like to form narratives, profits and wealth to convince new retail traders to buy their program that allegedly made them this fabricated wealth.

*The retail Broker*

A successful trader should have the same mindset and approach towards brokers as they should towards trading educators. One must first ask, where the conflict of interest lies. How does the retail broker make money? When trading stocks the broker will charge a commission for every executed order, so they receive money twice for every position the trader takes (Buying and selling/ opening and closing the position). So the retail broker, to maximize returns, will want to get you to place as many orders as possible, because more executed orders means more profits. This is the first major conflict of interest, as higher trading volume is not necessarily the best for the trader.

This leads to a bias in the education that brokers often provide to market their platform. They claim that their platform is better than the competition because they offer free education, tough the education only teaches you what is good for the broker. Since the broker wants as many executed trades as possible to maximize profit they will for example tell the retail broker that "overnight risk" as they call it, is always unfavorable and that you should close any position at the end of the trading day and not hold them overnight. In reality the risk of large gaps between trading days is usually very low to none, and very foreseeable because gaps are tied to big political  or economic events. By teaching the retail trader that overnight risk is bad, they are guaranteed two executions/payments per day, which is undeniably very appealing to them as said before.

When trading in foreign exchange, the broker makes money via the spread. For every executed order you pay a pip or more (percent in point) to enter the position. Since the value of one pip depends on the position size, the broker would like their costumer to trade with a good deal of volume and very often. Because of that, high leverage is obviously offered and readily available. Margin requirements can be as small as 1%, meaning a retail trader with only 1000$ can buy a full lot (100,000$) worth of currency resulting in a risk exposure of 10$ per pip and a good profit for the broker. Despite the profits a broker makes by offering you leverage, there is yet another catch: You pay interest on the leveraged volume, which incentivizes the broker to offer an even higher leverage. Unsurprisingly, foreign exchange and other markets of a similar nature are seemingly pushed and marketed more to the trader, often on the front page of the brokerage platform, that all conveniently make the broker more money.

Finally, assuming that 90% of traders lose money over their trades, the brokers will naturally want to take the other side of that position as a good method for them to hedge since they are the market makers in these type of markets; a concept that is sadly often very foreign to the retail trader. Them taking the other side of the trade understandably poses another conflict of interest with the trader. But retail brokers and trading educators are not the „bad guys", they aren't stealing money from the retail traders. They do what they are taught and that is to hedge and minimize risk while maximizing profit with anything they do. It is up to you not to let them take your money, by doing what is actually good for your account, and not what you were incentivized to do. Never risking more than your personal risk tolerance, usually far below 1% of your account in any given trade. It is very easy to calculate the risk of a portfolio and adjust it, as I will explain in a later chapter on risk management. The upside of the retail brokers are the massive provided liquidity. Just like volatility, it is imperative for the trader to have enough liquidity. But the 90% of traders that lose money, ironically only provide the professionals with the liquidity to enter a position in a good level.

*The institutional Trader*

Institutional traders are taught on day one to enter a trade at the right level or not enter at all. With bigger accounts and thus smaller liquidity it can take weeks to get the order filled and avoid pushing the price up. Usually the institutional trader will get into a position at the exact level where the retail traders decide to cut their losses and close their position by selling their shares to the institutional trader. This level is very predictable as it is usually a few points below the last resistance. Because of the misinformation from the trading educator and the lack of or misunderstanding of risk management, 90% of retail traders are ironically helping the institutional trader open their positions at favorable levels. As a calculated trader who goes into this sector for the long term and to make constant and strong profits, one must find the winners in the market and reproduce their actions.

What advantages do institutional traders have to retail traders? Since institutional traders seem to be the winners and we want to emulate them, we must find out what they do correctly and if they have an edge. Institutional traders can afford the technology to engage in strategies that a retail trader cannot, for example high frequency trading. Also since they can engage in direct market access, it is often assumed that they have an edge simply because they can see the order flow. They work in large teams and are often regulated by higher management, so they do not have the risk of making mistakes due to emotions. If an institutional trader goes through a bad time in their life and cannot control their emotions during trading which can hurt the performance, a supervisor or higher ranking individual will take notice of this and oblige the trader to take a holiday leave for example. However an institutional trader like a hedge fund manager or proprietary trader at an investment bank often look at retail traders as having the edge. Retail traders are not restricted to one asset class unless they restrict themselves, perhaps from seeing trading educators constantly branding themselves, unlike institutional traders that often are restricted to one asset due to their previous success and subsequent reputation in that asset class. Despite not being able to see order flow, a retail trader can fill a position just at the push of a button and usually gets all shares at the same level where exposure was wanted. For the institutional trader liquidity is a big issue, as filling the order too fast will push up the price of the security, and since they don't get filled at once the price might continue to move to less satisfactory levels while they are waiting to get filled. This also makes hedging more difficult. This is where the conflict of interest comes in, as it is now evident that entering at a good level is imperative for the institutional trader who works with high volume.

The retail trader is often taught by the trading educator to get into a position purely based on technical analysis and no fundamental reasons for the price moving. It might be a moving average crossing (this line crosses this line), a certain value of technical indicators or a chart pattern that has already formed. Since they wait for confirmation, a move in price has already happened when they enter the trade, and thus have to reduce risk by putting their stop price right underneath the previous resistance. Usually the price will retrace back to that previous resistance before continuing to rise, which means the retail trader is stopped out of the position. The institutional trader then uses this level to place their orders and get filled. This means that the institutional traders opens their position, exactly where the retail trader decides to cut losses and close the position. This is often called "stop hunting" in the retail world, meaning that the institutional traders will ask themselves at which level most retail traders will sell and close their positions, and use that level as their entry.

Going back to the beginning of the book, I said that successful traders are not just going to give you their money, they are looking at the same chart as the retail trader and since 90% of traders lose money, it means that most traders get into a position at the exact same very obvious level. It only takes two seconds to figure out where most people put their entry and exit levels, because they are always right above or below a resistance/ support level. A possible simple solution of many is, to just emulate the professional traders and put your entry price exactly where you would have put your exit level (Stop price). This means waiting for a pullback after the price crosses a psychologically important level like a resistance or moving average to enter the trade and not buy while the market is rising. Essentially doing the opposite of what trading educators and brokers often preach which is to "wait for confirmation" or in other words, wait until the move already happened. Market orders (buying at the current price whatever it currently is) is almost never a good idea. Instead a good trader will know where the price will go and place only limit orders below the current market price. Instead of having to cut losses, the entry is now at that level, which makes for less risk, more returns and a wider profit to risk ratio. With market orders, the amount of shares you want to buy are filled regardless of price. Every share might be bought at a different value and it cannot be estimated or predicted what those prices will be. It can be difficult to calculate the risk of a position and its volatility in advance when the trader does not know at what price they will get filled at.

*Market makers:*
Since short term trading is very profitable and preferable to retail brokers and trading educators, it is always a narrative that is being pushed as the ideal method and time frame in trading. The market makers also have a conflict of interest with the retail trader trading on the short term, and use that to make a profit with every order that is executed intraday.

Market makers provide liquidity to the markets by offering both sides of the trade. They profit with every executed order because of the difference in the bid-ask spread. A market maker might be a company specializing in providing liquidity, or it could be the brokerage itself. With derivatives like CFD's, the market maker being the broker might pose a conflict of interest with the trader, as they can see the order flow and levels that were set and subsequently move the price in a direction that is beneficial to the broker/market maker. In short, they are taking the other side of the trade that the client is taking or hedging against the clients side of the trade. Since there are no order costs in instruments like CFD's or spread betting, the bid-ask spreads are usually wider resulting in a losing out of the money position as soon as the trade is entered. Market makers see order flow and accounts in margin trouble. They can cause short or long squeezes in stop runs to trigger all stop loss orders set on obvious levels. They create weird candle patterns visible to intraday traders, that seem very unusual to them and might trigger emotions. A market maker can re-quote you as often as he wants and everyone who used trading software for foreign exchange will be familiar with the sentence "Do you accept these new quotes?". When taking out stop losses they can set a range to be taken out, where the price will spike up or down to a level where a lot of stops are located to fill these conditional orders, only to bounce back to the previous price right away. The market makers make their money mostly by the spread, which they can increase or decrease at will, for example during short periods of high volatility following a news event. Deviating from certain levels might cause traders to keep the position open for longer than they intended for example over a weekend, in which case the price may gap after the weekend in the first open. Often the market closes the gap where the price just retraces to the previous level before the gap which then triggers a lot of traders stop loss orders placed near that level. Some tactics that market makers use don't influence stock traders as much as they do to markets where leverage and short time frames are more common or even required. In foreign exchange the trader at a retail broker will have to use leverage for which high interest is paid, making a long term position less attractive. Additionally swaps and uncertainties during the weekend expose the trader to more unwanted risk.

# Chapter 2: Making a living

*Compounding*

In this chapter I will explain the reality of the industry and the job as a trader, and I will go into the specific mistakes that retail traders make due to bad education from people with a conflict of interest. The narrative that you can instantly quit your job and work as a day trader is simply not possible. A trader who is not part of the 90% that are losing, doesn't necessarily have to be making consistent profits to be in the 10%. The truth is that a much smaller percentage of people actually make a consistent return on the long term. Being in the 10% just means that you are not actively losing money. The amount of money one can make in a month clearly depends on the capital available, since being profitable in the long term means strict risk management and never risking more than the personal risk tolerance on any given trade. This makes over-leveraging a great risk to the safety of the portfolio, and means that one has to base their expected returns purely or mostly on their performance in relation to their capital.

Let's assume that a trader successfully beat the market and made 21% return in a year. This particular trader may require 40,000$ per year in income before tax to pay his bills, in which case his trading account needs to be at least 190,000$ for those 21% to cover the entire required yearly income. Of course the return on the very far end of the spectrum might be as high as doubling the account once a year, but that is very rare. Passive investing where one hedges the portfolio against market movement (Delta neutral portfolio), or simply relies on dividends for income might make only 3-8% per year. So unless large amounts of capital are ready to be used in the trading account one can't quit their job right away and simply rely on trading. The truth that all trading educators and social media traders fail to mention is that compounding plays a massive part of capital growth. A realistic way to generate enough income to rely on trading alone is to put part of the monthly paycheck into an account and trade profitably but conservatively in the markets without ever taking money out of the account. You are in this case supposed to leave the account alone, never take money out of the account, once it is inside it is gone. The new retail traders often cannot handle this fact and immediately think of ways to consume the money they made. The graph below illustrates the difference between the linear growth of an account where the money made is being taken out every month, compared to a chart of exponential growth when factoring in compounding once per month.

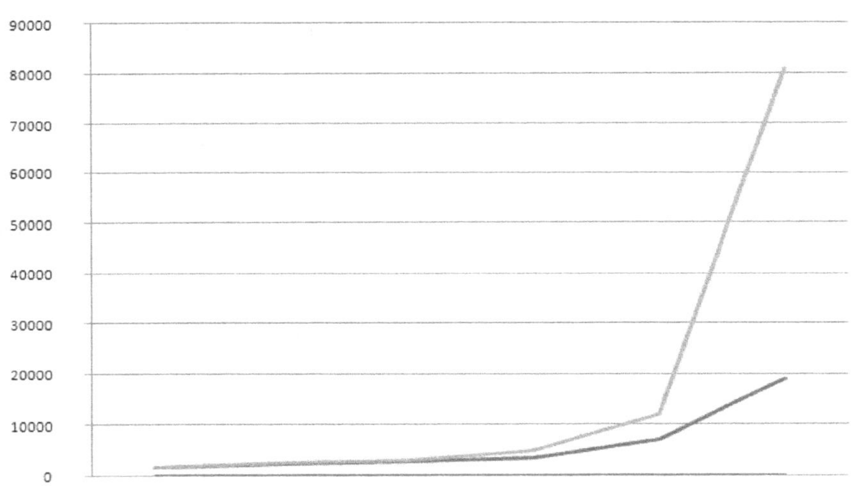

From the graph it is clearly visible that allowing the account to compound first before paying yourself a salary is crucial to capital growth. The minimal amount of capital required to finance a living with trading is based on your personal performance over years and salary required before tax, so it is very easy to know when the right time is to quit working and focus solely on trading. The reality is sadly not as glamorous as the fictional narrative that trading educators and the media like to form, but it is a lot more reasonable and perhaps less risky than being employed if done correctly. It will take months to learn and practice to trade, months to learn the discipline and years to learn how to control emotions. It might take years to accumulate the capital to finally rely solely on trading for a living but the only thing required for it is a modicum of patience and common sense.

*Long term investments*
Apart from the standard get rich quick model, the far other side is very long term investment, such as a 30 year time frame. The power of a fully passive approach of investing cannot be underestimated. Imagine a 30 year old investing 10,000$ once, and never touching it again until exactly 30 years are over. The average annual return of the S&P500 has been slightly over 11% annually. Assuming this annual return and factoring in annual compounding, that investment of a mere 10,000$ would be worth about 230,000$ in 30 years with no work at all during those 30 years. If that same person invested an additional 50$ every month, the account would be worth 355,000$ after the

same amount of time. From this we can see not only the importance of compounding and general discipline but also the importance of not tampering with the funds or taking money out of the account for momentary spending.

*Time frames*

I already briefly mentioned some of the major mistakes retail traders make, which result in losing more than half of their trades and I will briefly sum them up before getting into additional mistakes. Retail traders often restrict themselves to a short timeframe, only looking at the 30m or the 1h candle chart. They think that overnight risk is bad due to fear of gaps and overnight interest because of high leverage that they took. They don't go with the performance of the market but instead with the confirmation biased instinct to close a position at the end of the day. When the timeframe that is being looked at gets shorter and the move that a trader is trying to profit from is getting smaller, the difficulty of predicting the market direction goes up and the traders hit rate will go down when the time frame that is being looked at gets smaller. It is this way with every trader, regardless of experience. A new trader should therefore perhaps start with the weekly candles and predict a move over the next few months. This reduces the profitability of the trade since compounding isn't factored in and a lot of patience is required which retail traders typically lack. They want to see results right away. After experiencing reasonable success in predicting long term movements one can only then move to smaller time frames like one week or less per position. To Day-trade the market must simply provide the necessary volatility, which is rarely the case and certainly not every day. The second thing retail traders often restrict themselves to is an asset class as I previously mentioned in another chapter. A trader has the opportunity to profit from all asset classes, that even an institutional trader does not have due to them having a good reputation in one asset class. A retail trader can simply go where the markets are moving whether it is stocks, commodities, currencies or other securities, so it makes no sense for them to restrict themselves to one asset class. Remember that the most important thing when trying to be profitable and make a living of trading is to make constant profits whatever the market situation currently is like. Despite all that a trader might have a good understanding of a specific strategy that he developed and will use this strategy as often as the market allows and keep refining it. Some institutional traders argue that constantly changing ones trading strategy is a big contributing factor in retail traders not making money. Thus, it Is important to differentiate between "system hopping" and restricting oneself to a certain asset class or time frame. A trader may have good expertise in one specific asset class and choose to allocate most of their capital to that asset class within their portfolio. When the market goes down, they try to profit by being net short in their portfolio. When volatility becomes high but market direction is too unpredictable they may use derivatives and simultaneous trading of the underlying asset to create a delta neutral portfolio and simply trade volatility. When the particular asset class does not move at all or does not provide enough volatility for a good profit, the trader might hedge to only trade the absence of volatility using options hedging strategies. So while it is very possible to be successful in trading almost only one asset class, this requires a lot of experience and should never be something which traders decide before or right after they start trading.

## Pseudo-scammers

The main problem with most new traders losing money is simply the vast majority of deliberately wrong information and outright scams on the internet. This is twofold; an outright scam can be a trader advertising a trading system for a substantial amount of money. Logically this sort of system cannot exist, as a trader with a successful black box system will want to keep it for himself. If it is profitable he would not need to sell it to other people and would not want that as it will be rendered useless very fast. Another useless service that charlatans will try to sell are trading "signals", where they request far more money than one can make from their system to get their recommendations for trades and levels for entry and exit. These often have a low hit-rate and are designed for only a very specific time frame and risk tolerance that might not be suitable for every trader. When the information is not an outright scam, it is often deliberately false to push a narrative that's only beneficial to the other party. Educators like to advocate for tight stop-losses and waiting for confirmation before entering a trade. The problem with waiting for confirmation is firstly missing the move entirely if it takes place on the short term, and an increase in risk or decrease in the risk-profit ratio meaning that when entering trades only where the move has already happened, the amount of risk compared to the amount of potential profit gets bigger, resulting in less profitability over the long term.

# Chapter 3: Emotions

A big part of trading, that is often not mentioned in the media is emotional control and certain personality traits that successful traders have. A retail trader will often go into trading based on the inaccurate portrayals in finance movies in which traders are shown very passionate about their short term positions acting like gamblers on a high roll in a casino. They go into trading getting emotional about losses and profits and directly connect the profits to materialistic things, like what they can spend the money on. Imagine holding a specific number of cash in your hand that you made over two days trading the markets, say 1200$. What does that money mean to you? Most people will connect it to paying off materialistic things that they purchased like a car or even luxury goods which they don't necessarily need. The truth is that the 1200$ in profit are more capital to fund growth and a higher return the next month. When a trader makes 10%, then the 1200$ that were made promise a 120$ higher return for the next 10% if kept in the trading account, which is then also compounded. The value amount made through trading should not matter as much as the percentage increase in account capital as growth of capital and subsequent growth of income are the only important factors in making consistent profits in the markets. Personality traits of traders require a lot of learning similar to practicing an instrument or a sport. It requires a lot of discipline and continuous repetitions, each time learning to react to certain situations in the right way. In a way this is pure training of the personality as opposed to the technical factors involved in trading that are just personal guidelines that one has to follow. The trader must be confronted by difficult situations and still be able to maintain important personality traits such as discipline in sticking to the predetermined levels, rules, guidelines and simultaneous flexibility when required to change ones view if it turned out to be biased due to emotions.

*Adding to a losing trade*

It is easy to become a victim of one's emotions and fall into the trap of gambling-like behavior in the markets. A typical mistake of this nature is adding into a losing trade. From an outside perspective it can be hard to see why a retail traders makes many of the mistakes he makes and is very different from actual trading. A trading educator will often suggest to start paper trading, meaning not buying securities with actual money but instead simulating the trade on paper to practice the actual strategy. However only when trading with real money and risk do ones emotional responses become apparent. All of the sudden it is not so easy to stick to the same disciplines and it becomes very tempting if untrained, to avoid the confirmation biases and mistakes that resemble gambling like behavior.

Imagine, a trade is placed and the asset moves the opposite direction of the speculated or desired one. The retail trader sees the money being lost and that dreaded red minus sign before a constantly rising figure. This evokes an emotional response which can differ in nature from person to person. Some might have the urge to instantly panic sell the entire position, while others might have the exact opposite reaction. The problem with the first is that they didn't stick to their plan, and now might be selling because of random "noise" in the markets or because of a temporary move that will return to normal levels in the next candle. The latter response results in the "two for one" mentality, where the trader falls into bias and convinces himself that the decline in share price or move against his speculated direction is a positive outcome. The trader might be tempted to buy more shares in a security that is moving against him, because he thinks that now he can get more profit if it goes back up, and enter at a more favorable level. The problem is twofold. Firstly the likelihood of the price going to the target profit level is now steadily reducing, and the hit-rate or success rate is therefore declining. The other problem is that when buying more, it is essentially a new and different trade. The speculated levels and price movement has turned out to be wrong already, and buying again just creates a new trade that now risks having a stop level that is too low, and very likely to be reached by just random movements in the market not indicative of any trend in price. it is not thought out well and just breaks the discipline.

The bias caused by emotions that tempts a trader to add to a losing trade can also be triggered by the trader viewing the money as already lost, as soon as the red minus sign appears. While a steady decline in price over a certain amount of time can be indicative of a losing trade, a small tick against the speculated direction is not necessarily meaningful. To differentiate between meaningful and meaningless moves, the trader could simply stick to level that was decided before entering the trade and avoid emotions factoring into decisions that way. Failing to do so, and viewing the money as lost, can result in gambling behavior as well by tempting the trader to make even bigger trades to be able to make up for losses or at least break even. This can manifest by adding money into a losing trade to make the position bigger and therefore increase the upside. As said before, this not only results in the downside being increased at least as much, but also reducing the likelihood of that trade, or in other words it reduces the chance of the trade succeeding, simply because the distance to the stop level is now closer and random noise in the markets has a bigger effect.

*Discipline, bias and emotions*
Emotions during trading play a big part in causing confirmation bias when analyzing a stock. Even institutional traders can describe incidents, where they

held on to a losing stock that kept falling for years despite that stock already passing the predetermined levels for exit and cutting losses. They might describe it as being in love with a stock, where due to confirmation bias the trader is blind to the obvious signs that the trade is a losing position. Therefore it is easy to conclude that emotional control is very important in finance and especially the stock market.

I will describe a scenario that illustrates why it is crucial to stick to the predetermined rules. This is where discipline comes in to prevent unaccounted losses. Before any position the trader needs to know all possible outcomes, profit made and money lost. Discipline is especially hard to follow when there is an emotional reason not to follow the previously decided guidelines. These emotions are often unreasonable but still hard to ignore. For example a company that went insolvent while trading at 200$ crashes to below 1$. It would take 19900% in growth before that stock reaches its previous price to prevent losses and reach breakeven, which is usually impossible. Furthermore, there are most likely fundamental reasons for the company to never operate as previously again. A retail trader might get into this situation despite deciding to close the position at a certain level, say 192$ because when the level was crossed to 191$ the trader was uncomfortable with taking an unexpectedly bigger loss, so they decided to wait for an upwards movement to sell at the predetermined level. This level never comes and the company due to fundamental reasons continuous to fall but the trader keeps reevaluating and due to confirmation bias forms narratives to tell himself that the stock will at some point change direction again. In this situation the trader was ready to risk 4% of the position (which should be less than 1% of their whole account), but ended up losing 99.5% of the money invested in that position. This should illustrate very well how a tiny infraction of discipline can lead to a total loss of the invested money in a position and prove that very strict discipline in emotional control, and sticking to the predetermined rules is crucial, for which there should never be any exceptions. This scenario also perfectly shows natural human behavior and why discipline and following rules even if set by the person that is following them is important. Aside from the financial world, this kind of emotional control is used in many other industries like aviation in which pilots and especially air traffic controllers are constantly monitored by psychologists during training to detect susceptibility to stress and emotions. They are trained to follow "sterile cockpit" rules during take-off for example in which friendly chatter and anything not strictly connected to their work is not allowed. In the financial world this might be the case in higher ranking positions some even taking MRI scans to determine susceptibility to emotions in trading. In other cases the higher ranking supervisor will monitor the traders emotional state and might decide to force a holiday leave if the trader seems too stressed and unable to perform his tasks without involving emotions. In retail trading there is obviously no one to regulate the trader so the retail trader has to be especially careful since an unbiased self reflection is very difficult. It is therefore crucial for the retail trader to stick to discipline when trading. Rules that are set might be technical like sticking to certain levels for buying and selling, but might also be related to personality. For example deciding never to trade when one did not get enough sleep the night before, otherwise the quality of the work might suffer. If you work in a hedge fund and come to work visibly sick, tired or hung-over, the supervising manager would not want you to be exposed to their clients risk, and would most likely send you home for the day. When trading with one's own money, the trader has to be especially careful about evaluating ones capability to perform the required tasks on any given day. A trader might also decide never to trade unless completely sober. If no complete discipline is followed a similar scenario might ensure to the previously described one, where the line gets blurred. A trader might make an exception after only having had half a drink, but then it is unclear after how many drinks it is irresponsible to keep trading because the line that was previously set was already crossed. Similar rules might be to not trade when dealing with strong emotional distress due to the passing of a loved one for example. In conclusion, self awareness and introspection is absolutely necessary at all times.

Next to discipline and emotional control, another very important trait for a trader is an almost cynical drive in the markets. There is no room for naivety in the markets, because a trader is up against everyone else, and there are some very intelligent participants in the market. The vast majority of false information or outright scams available on the internet like to claim that the retail trader is up against "dumb money" and that just a little risk management is enough to win against them. Aside from the fact that the risk management that is taught is often deliberately false as stated in the previous chapters (pushing short term trading and tight stops for example), the message itself is misleading. A market maker will take a retail trader out for a single pip and they can see which accounts are in margin trouble. Besides the market maker, a retail trader is up against the algorithms made by the most intelligent academics you can think of. This includes people with doctorates in quantum physics and rocket science or very renowned mathematicians. Some advanced hedge funds will spend hundreds of millions to lay cables over the city to their office, just to have an advantage in the nanoseconds and take advantage of their formulated algorithms. A retail trader is up against high frequency trading and algorithms that were built only to predict what trade another algorithm will take. Then there are algorithms that predict the algorithms that predict other algorithms. Even if you are not trading on the short term, you might be trailing a stop and still have the constant risk of getting taken out of the market or the market becomes seemingly unpredictable and cause a retail trader to close the position before the trend just resumes.

## The right mindset

After stressing the importance of discipline and emotional control I want to describe what it means if a trader does not have this mindset, which is something a lot of retail traders experience. What is a trader who constantly puts money into the market, gets excited over every position, happy when they make money and feel negative when they lose money? This is by definition a gambler, not a trader. A trader without any discipline and emotional control is in no way different from a gambler at a casino no matter how allegedly good a traders strategy or system is. When not sticking to predetermined risk and other disciplines the following scenarios might take place that result in addictive behavior and perhaps even a pseudo gambling addiction even though the market is no place for this kind of behavior. A trader makes three big wins in a row (see chapter one about clusters) and gets overly confident. The trader decides to have a big bet after concluding that his system is so successful that a bigger position won't hurt in the long term. Additionally the trader is thinking that he is too small in his winning positions and day dreams about the large amounts of profit he would have made if he invested his entire account into those last winning positions. The trader forgets that even though these three particular trades would have made a good profit if he invested more than he calculated for his risk tolerance, this would not be sustainable in the long term and there is no way of knowing if a trade will perform exactly as expected before opening the position. After taking a bigger position than on the three winning trades, the trader now looses everything he made in those three winners. Usually a trader is very focused on his risk to profit ratio, where a winning trade always makes a lot more than a losing trade risks. But because he broke his discipline just once after a string of good luck, he was three times bigger on his risk than his reward in the last trade.

A very similar scenario with the same potential for losses but reversed is the following scenario: A trader has a string of "bad luck" three times in a row. This seems worse than it is because it happens on average every eight trades in a

50% system and even in a respectable 75% hit rate system it is a common occurrence. With a gambling mentality the trader will feel stress and general unease from the loss and tries to make the money back fast by increasing position sizing and therefore also risk. Since the risk is increased and no longer ideal and sustainable on the long term the trader will make a guaranteed loss in two scenarios; either the next position is winning and some but not all of the losses of the previous three trades are made back in which case the trader will get a false sense of market approval and continue his mismanaged risk calculations until he blows his account, or the trader looses on the next position as well making the total loss now too big to recover. The trader panics further and this repeats itself until the account is blown as well. A big problem with losses is the misunderstanding of percentages. If someone offered a trader 20,000$ for 1% of his company, then changed his bid to 20,000$ for 2%, how much more of the company does he want? Here it is not 1% more but 100%. It is important to differentiate between percentage points and the actual percentage. If a stock halves to 50$, then 100$ is double of 50, so the stock needs to gain 100% again. This means that a 5% fall in price of a security does not necessarily mean, 5% in the other direction brings the position back to breakeven. In fact this is so overlooked that traders who previously blew an account just start from breakeven when refunding the account, when it should start at a negative value. Since recovering from losses takes more movement than making profit, it should be obvious that protecting capital and profits from losses is a high priority in trading and the opposite of a gambling mentality. I will explain more on percentage calculation in a later chapter.

*Broken rules*

After exceptions were made and rules were broken the trader often finds himself either very stressed by the losses and engaging in gambling-like behavior to desperately make the profits back or very keen of the emotional excitement that comes from trading similar to a player at a casino. In this mindset consistent profits are impossible and any profits would instantly be given back to the markets. Many financial derivatives seem to cause this effect in traders, because the margin requirements are so small that only a very small amount of money invested is needed for big returns and risk. The hit rate in these financial derivatives is usually extremely low and the time frames are so short that the market direction is unpredictable. This behavior is not only appealing but required as using the leveraged capital overnight often has unaffordable amounts of interest attached to it. Because of that many traders find themselves engaging in gambling behavior. To sum up, these derivatives offer a very low chance of winning a lot of money with very little money put in, in a short amount of time. How is this any different from a slot machine? Obviously derivatives are not made to steal money from the retail trader, in fact they are usually instruments where the market maker is the broker himself, so the institutional traders don't even gain liquidity from other peoples bad positions. For the institutional trader derivatives are not instruments to increase risk exposure and higher profits in the markets, but tools for a very specific purpose. With options you could for example hedge delta of the portfolio to a neutral or delta zero portfolio, in which the market direction has no impact at all on profits or losses. Instead they offer exposure to volatility itself.  Therefore derivates serve a complex purpose and are not simply meant for increasing profits and using them for the high leverage in gambling like behavior.

*Fear of missing out and loss aversion*
Another common issue that traders face, further shows the importance of emotional control. The fear of missing out often called 'FOMO' constitutes a large amount of loosing trades made by retail traders. After a big move it is usually not the best time to buy an asset because the stop losses set by most traders will be slightly below the level where the big move started. Usually as described in previous chapters the price will retrace to that price before the move and trigger all the stops. This is also often called a fake breakout by retail traders, in which the price rapidly pushes up through a known resistance and motivates retail traders to buy the stock at that exact price. The problem is that institutional traders see the very same chart that retail traders are looking at. They will set their limit orders right at the stop level of the retail traders, and get the liquidity when the price pulls back again to the previous price to capitalize from the real breakout move.

On the other side, although less prevalent, trades may suffer from loss aversion following a string of losses as they have become sensitive to further losses or following a string of successful trades as they become very protective of the profits and experience an aversion to giving them back to the market. Loss aversion will cause the exact opposite as the fear of missing out and prevent the trader from entering possibly profitable trades to prevent any losses. The result is the same as with fear of missing out, which is reduced profitability. The only way to prevent these feelings and not fall into a bias is to constantly evaluate ones previous positions and statistics to see if profitability was reduced. When profitability changes between quarters or months, it is important to catch any divergence or convergence between profitability and factors such as trading frequency. When trading frequency drastically decreases and profitability decreases in a similar manner, one can conclude from this convergence, that there is a relation between the two and it is worth asking if it is a technical or emotional issue like loss aversion that is causing the reduced profitability of the portfolio. Similarly the statistics of a portfolio can show divergences such as Profitability increasing with decreasing trading frequency displaying a link that could possibly mean that the trader is now choosing his positions more effectively. Whatever the divergence or convergence may be, a trader should analyze these often and derive the reasoning behind the changes.

*Hyperbolic discounting*
Many fall into the trap off trying to get rich fast, increasing their risk tolerance and falling into the gambling mindset. Hyperbolic discounting is a phenomena where a person prefers a smaller immediate reward over a bigger reward that is further in the future. It is human nature that immediate acquisition increases the chances of survival. Out in the wild a piece of food now might be better than two pieces in a week.

However one should not have to rely solely on the money made in trading. The problem with living month to month off the trading profits is that when a month arrives where the profit was much lower than what is needed that month, then the total capital gets lowered as well in that month. Since the profit per month is based in percent of the account and not as a standalone value this will result in the next months profit being lower as well, which is another reason why we all hear of people who lost everything in the markets. They simply had to withdraw the same amount every month to live, while the profits kept shrinking due to the capital being tampered with.

Ideally the money should be seen as gone once it is in the trading account and only there to keep growing until it can be decided that a certain cut of those profits can be paid every month for some extra spending money. When the wage that one withdraws from the trading account each month is not life saving and absolutely necessary, it will greatly help to eliminate emotional biases like hyperbolic discounting.

The risk of this phenomenon in trading can manifest itself in different ways. The trader might be tempted upon seeing that the position went the speculated way to close the position right away and take the in that moment guaranteed profits rather than risk, that the position might go the other way and turn those small but guaranteed profits into a loss. On the other side one might be tempted to close a position long before the decided stop level, because they think that it cannot turn around at this point and want to avoid taking an even bigger loss than the guaranteed smaller number that they are seeing at that current moment. This is a major deviation from the planned way the trade would go, and results in a constantly lowering level of discipline that if spiraled out of control leads to gambling behavior. When a trade is planned and two exit levels are assigned (a stop and profit level), one has to force themselves to stick to those levels and not fall victim to biases like hyperbolic discounting. What is the point in limiting the downside of a trade, if they are not going to stick to the minimum calculated upside?

*Stress and growth*

Despite sticking to the rules and the personal risk tolerance, a trader might find himself not able to sleep at night, and stressed during the day. In this state trading is impossible as emotions, especially stress need to be kept under control and ideally completely switched off during trading. A good way of dealing with stress associated with risk is by reducing position size and from there, recalculate the risk of the portfolio. Perhaps, change the total amount of risk to the portfolio by permanently reducing the risk tolerance until comfort is being felt from seeing the success of the trading strategy. Risk and decisions should be made based on facts and mathematical principles, in a way that is completely binary and void of emotional influence. That way the if the numbers are right, there is no need for personal judgment and therefore ideally no room for discomfort or stress. The trader decided on a risk beforehand and assuming that every calculation was done correctly, there should be no need in worrying about the potential loss. Perhaps it is a beneficial exercise to view the money as gone as soon as the trade is placed, since the risk was calculated and deemed acceptable anyway beforehand. There are obviously mathematical factors involved in finding the ideal amount of risk per portfolio to optimize growth, but more on that will be in the next chapter. To conclude, emotional control and discipline are just as crucial to trading as the mathematical and analytical side. To comfort the trader, he can recalculate the risks taken and the overall risk of the portfolio to reassure himself that everything was done right prior to executing the trade, and that there is no way for unexpected losses beyond the risk he was willing to take. If everything else fails, perhaps a gradual reduction in risk tolerance can benefit the trader, as it limits emotions factoring into decisions and therefore limits downside. Remember that by successfully concentrating on limiting downside for a long period of time will automatically lead to a growing upside.

# Chapter 4: Risk and management

*Leverage and liquidity*

The reputation of the stock market and trading in general is generally that of a very risky business and most people will view the occupation as a more risky one than being employed. But if you compare two people each successful in their fields you realize that a trader makes a living out of the capital he has in different equities. A person who is employed will depend on his firms wellbeing and his monthly income to pay for equities. These equities like real estate, at least the house they live in are usually more difficult to liquidate in times of money problems such as reduced working hours or being made redundant due to the company having capital problems completely unrelated to the person employed. A trader can usually liquidate equities more easily and since the income is based on capital, there will be spare capital in times of money problems. Furthermore the likelihood of a trader experiencing money problems is far less than that of an employed individual. As I described in a previous chapter the trader can take potentially take advantage of any market situation whether it is rising or falling, moving quickly with high volatility or not moving at all. The only thing a trader needs is liquidity, where an employed person cannot quickly change into another sector or field of expertise since his education or training will usually be in only one field. Most people have heard of traders and investors loosing most or all of their money in a financial crisis, which created the myth that traders are always at risk of losing everything at once. Why does this happen to some people? Aside from the lack of preparedness for such a scenario, the main problem is that income for a trader is based on their return and their capital. When return for any reason pauses during a financial crisis, but for obvious reasons their expenses don't stop, then the capital will continue decreasing resulting in the income decreasing. This goes on until a point is reached where the capital is so low that the income is lower than the expenses of the trader. Since a house is not always easy to liquidate, the trader may be unable to reduce their expenses to stop this slow decrease in capital. To avoid such a scenario a trader or investor needs to constantly monitor the relation between their spending and income, and ideally optimize growth and compounding  for the capital to not only stay above a certain level, but to keep growing. A meaningful mistake some retail traders make is getting into full time trading too early. Even though they may have enough capital and a good return to afford living only from trading, they might have missed to account for financial crisis and not experiencing any returns for multiple months in a row. Aside from getting into full time trading at the right time, watching the portfolio growth and creating prognosis, the scenario of no income needs to be avoided, trained and prepared for. Technically speaking a financial crisis should be no reason for a trader to stop making returns, in fact it should drastically increase returns because the volatility of the market usually goes up. One needs to be able to adapt quickly and train this skill of the potential of a market crash. For a good trader, there should be no technical reason for large losses at once and no reason for continuous lack of returns. A possible realistic reason for a scenario in which a trader stops making returns for months is emotional or health issues, mental issues or stress. In periods like these it may be impossible for the trader to make money and therefore start losing all his capital over a period of time. Compared to a person who is employed at a company and depends on his monthly wage, a trader will only slowly lose capital until bankruptcy, where the employee will likely have much less money saved up to accommodate for a time of physical or mental illness.

*Importance of risk management and calculations*

Not being in the 90% of traders that lose money in the markets does not mean that one is profitable. Even if not only no money is being lost, but also trades are consistently right, the trader might make little to no profit. There are many reasons for the risk reward being off. some can be deliberate before even entering the trade, and some can happen due to lapses in discipline during an open position. When more than half of the trades are winning positions, one would think that it results in a net positive outcome for the portfolio and money being made, but in reality the risk reward plays one of the biggest parts in the final outcome. Imagine that almost all trades are winners, and only a few are losses. If those losses then are multiple times larger than the profits made from the copious amount of winning trades, the trader obviously still loses money. The risk reward ratio, even in a system where more than half of all trades are winners, should be more than one to one, meaning every profit made should be larger than every loss made. Since profit always varies, and is practically unrestricted, one must limit the downside of the trade to increase the effects from the upside. Ideally a risk tolerance is decided in percent of the portfolio and every trade has a maximum loss not exceeding this value. For example a 0.75% risk tolerance on the portfolio would mean that all trades at any given time cannot result in a loss of greater than 0.75% of the total capital. The upside/profit is of course not limited, and the risk reward ratio is favorable. Of course, the expected profit from every trade is different and even though the risk is hedged, the stop is still placed where it reasonably needs to be. For that reason, the risk reward ratio cannot be the same for every trade since the two levels are placed with no relation to each other. The stop simply needs to be where it should be and the profit level if not trailing, needs to be at a reasonable level and not any level relative to the stop as long as it makes the trade look worth placing. Since the risk reward are dynamic in this way, one should rather decide whether to place a trade or not based on the risk reward ratio and not the opposite way.

The stop and take profit levels are decided first independently from each other, and only then should be decided if the ratio fits into the portfolio and trading strategy.

If the majority of trades are winning trades, but the losses are bigger than the profits, the trader might find himself losing money on a perhaps winning system. This can be caused by not sticking to the predetermined levels, thinking the price will go back up if the trader just waits. This kind of bargaining can even happen before placing the order of a trade, in the planning stage. In this case the trader might convince himself that even though the trade looks bad on paper and might have a low/close to one to one ratio on the risk reward, the hit-rate is likely so high and the position is a "sure thing" that the trader enters the position because of bargaining and risks not only damage to his discipline but to the long term success of the portfolio. One exception will lead to many, since this kind of thinking will never be an isolated incident, and the overall performance of the portfolio will severely decline. Soon the trader finds himself placing trades in which the losses are either the same or even outweigh the profit.

Even with more than half of the trades winning, this system will lead to monetary losses.

Even when proper discipline is being exercised in sticking to the predetermined stop loss level, a trader might find himself due to reasons mentioned earlier such as hyperbolic discounting, not sticking to the predetermined take profit level and closing the position early for smaller but guaranteed profit. Because of this, the actual risk reward ratio is different in the long term and unpredictable. The trader might think that every winning trade makes twice as much money than what is being lost in a losing trade, but in reality the risk reward ratio might be closer to one meaning that since the trades are often being closed early, the actual profit is just as much or less as the losses on a losing trade. The trader now makes no money despite an overwhelming amount of winning positions, that should have resulted in an overall profit.

*How to hedge*

Next to knowing the breakeven beforehand, it is crucial to know the breakeven of the trade before entering it. While the risk reward ratio might give the trader information on if a trade will be profitable in the long term for the portfolio, the breakeven gives a more individual insight on the current moment. When trading in foreign exchange, the broker makes their money trough the difference in the bid ask spread. The same goes for options and other derivatives. Once the trade is placed, it cannot be immediately closed again for the same level since the buying and selling price are slightly different. This is usually a small amount during normal market conditions, but during times of great volatility, especially following large news or political events, the gap will widen between the two quotes as a means for the market maker to hedge. The trader can either be in a position where they are buying because of a news event and are therefore at risk of entering a position during a wide bid ask spread, or enter the position during such an event unaware of the very recent news. Even though a position might have been planned over a larger time frame, the trader might miss out on profits or increase risk unwittingly, because they were unaware of the current bid ask spread. It is therefore necessary to factor in the spread and calculate a break even in addition to calculating the risk reward, and of course the stop and take profit levels.

In the stock market for example where the spread is usually not as volatile and wide as in the derivatives market, there is an additional fee to be factored in, which is the commission fee of the broker. With stocks as an example, the broker makes their profit through commission fees or provisions instead of through the bid ask spread, since they are providing not the service of liquidity directly but the service of routing the trade through an exchange. Imagine a trader with the same risk tolerance as in the previous example of 0.75%. Assuming that this trader has a trading account of 10,000$, this results in a total risk of 75$. Now let's assume that the broker charges 15$ per trade. Technically that money should be viewed as an instant loss, that needs to be made up for with the profits of that trade to breakeven. In reality, the trader is now risking 15$ on top of the 75$ with a total risk of 90$, thereby once again reducing the risk reward ratio. The actual risk, after entering the trade is now about 0.90% of the portfolio. Since fees, spreads and similar are unavoidable, one needs to factor in these amounts before entering the trade to have a clear image of the risk of this position and the impact on the portfolio in the long term.

When deciding a risk tolerance of the portfolio it is important to differentiate between the risk of a single position and the combined risk of the entire portfolio. If every trade is entered with the same dollar amount of risk relative to the capital of the account, then the risk although hedged, will still add up with every trade. If instead every trade is limited to a fraction of the total risk at a set value, then another problem occurs, which is a limitation on the maximum amount of concurrent trades. For example, with a risk tolerance of 1% of the portfolio and every trade being at a fragment of 0.20% risk, it would result in a portfolio where a maximum of five concurrent trades can be active at once. Additionally, limiting the risk of every trade to the same amount might pose inefficiencies in the management of the portfolio, as the size of the position is not based on its profitability. Trades with longer time frames, higher expected returns and most importantly a larger risk reward ratio are weighted the exact same as less profitable trades in this case. Ideally, the trades that look the best on paper or at least have the best expected profit to loss ratio should be favored. Although the risk allocation could be more efficient than with this method, it does successfully limit the maximum risk while helping to stay disciplined as the risk is always the same, the amount of trades at once are also limited, and a clear image of the total risk becomes easy to tell at any given moment.

There is no correct way to assign risk for individual trades. Some successful traders prefer to hedge the risk to a predetermined value for every trade, and just let the risk stack up, because they are hoping that the positive risk reward ratio and hit-rate of above 50% will result in good profitability and reasonable risk. This method is less time consuming and labor intensive. The drawback is that the risk can stack up to a technically unlimited amount as there is no way to calculate a maximum amount of trades. Seeing multiple trades that are in the red can trigger an emotional response to enter even more trades and the calculated risk being hedged on every trade can lure the trader into a false sense of security. They believe that since the risk of a position is capped and hedged every time that they are safe from unexpected losses, but it is easy in a method like this to lose situational awareness of the portfolio and end up with the majority of the entire capital being inadvertently at risk. The previously mentioned advantage of this method now becomes distorted as it takes more and more workload to keep the overall situation clear. To be on top of the current risk to the capital, the overall risk needs to be recalculated after every consecutive trade is placed and judgment is required every time to determine whether the risk is at a reasonable level or not, obviously risking emotional bias factoring into the decision. This method as said before is not right or wrong and up to the trader, however one should be aware of every possibility that could cloud judgment and influence bias and discipline. In a completely binary system, there is no need for judgment, and only yes or no answers prevail in the decision making progress. whichever strategy is being pursued, it is crucial to keep judgment to a minimum and ideally make every process a mathematical yes or no answer to prevent emotions from influencing decisions.

A further drawback of this method is that it breaks the discipline. When judgment is required to make any decision instead of a mathematical yes or no answer, the trader as mentioned before runs into the risk of making decisions in which emotions and bias factored in. Every time emotions are given a chance to cloud judgment, there is a risk of the discipline being broken. It could be the smallest mistake that ends up leading into a downward spiral to ever decreasing discipline, and should therefore be avoided as much as possible. Good introspection and honesty with one's self is absolutely crucial to ensuring success in the long term.

The other method in which the decided risk applies to the entire portfolio is to hedge every position and weigh it relative to the combined risk of the whole portfolio. A bigger position will have a greater impact on the total amount of risk to the portfolio before it is hedged and inversely with a smaller position. While the amount of shares or the dollar amount of the value of those combined shares can all be hedged to the same amount of risk, it could be beneficial to have a higher risk allocated to positions that are expected to yield more money due to a higher risk reward ratio. A position in which three times more profit is expected than risk, might be better than a position where only 1.5 times the amount of profit compared to losses are expected. With a steady hit rate, favoring these positions might lead to an increase in profit over the long term for the trader. Additionally to the risk reward ratio, another favorable trait of a position is the hit rate. Although it cannot be predicted if the speculated direction that the stock will trade will be right, the hit rate often goes up with longer time frames. Factoring this in, a position with a higher expected time frame and a higher expected risk reward ratio might be favored over shorter, uncertain and low profitability trades, and allocated more risk. This could be allocating 0.5% risk per position when it looks better on paper and only allocating 0.2% of risk to that position of it is not as favorable but still worth doing according to the calculations. With this method judgment is once again often required to decide what trade should be favored and therefore weighted more, and there is once again a risk of emotions factoring into the judgment, leading to unfavorable decisions. Additionally, even if done strictly mathematically, it cannot be decisively known in advance how a trade will perform and often a trade that looked unprofitable on paper can yield a much higher return than what was expected. Unfortunately this would lead to some trades that were weighted less and deemed to be less profitable than others, to perform well but create a lot less profit than what could have been made, if the positions where all weighted equally.

It cannot be understated how important it is to know the exact risk to the capital before entering a position. Limiting risk is the only thing that matters to sustain the portfolio. Even a portfolio that never makes any money is better than a portfolio that loses all of its money, as is the case with 90% of retail traders. Knowing the risk will help to hedge against it and reduce it in the future. if it is done only after the trades and the losses are simply catalogued, there will never be a time where those statistics are useful since the account already lost all of its money before little tweaks to increase performance can even be considered.

*Understanding percentage calculation*
Understanding how percentage especially changes in percentage works is key to avoiding bargaining as an emotional response. Seeing a stock drop 10%, one might instinctively think that it only needs to go up 10% to be at the same level again. This leads to bargaining where a person convinces himself that by just waiting he can make up for losses and hold on to a losing stock for longer than

he intended to. The reality is that to make up for a 10% drop, the asset must rise 11.1% again to be at the same value. Imagine a stock halving in value, so a reduction of 50%. To reach the same level again as before the halving it needs to double, and not increase by 50% again. Since it needs to double it requires growth of 100% its current price to be at the same price again. An example with monetary values would be a stock that is bought at 100$ per share that drops by 50%. It is now at 50$. To get back to the entry level of 100$ it needs to rise 100% or 50$, since 50$ are 100% of 50$.

This is crucial to keep in mind to have realistic expectations and not fall victim to clouded judgment that forms unrealistic expectations and leads to unhealthy decisions.

This understanding of percentage calculation or lack of understanding plays a big role in the losses that often occur when trading penny stocks. People go into penny stock trading with the mindset that it poses an incredible opportunity, since if the stock at 0.1$ went up to "only" 1$, then the trader would tenfold their investment. It can seem very deceptively lucrative and realistic that a stock would rise to 1$ since it is such a low amount and there are a substantial amount of stocks far over that one dollar mark. However that seemingly reasonable growth is a factor of 10 meaning 1000% of the starting price which is incredible unreasonable and rare. The risk of a trade like this is obviously still the same as with every other trade since it depends on the money invested and the downside which is always from 0-100% regardless of the price, however the likelihood of making the expected profit is essentially zero. It is almost no different than playing the lottery and uses the same "but what if" mindset that completely ignores the realistic chances of succeeding. Besides the unrealistic expectation of growth, there is not enough volatility simply because of the laws of supply and demand and not enough interest in that specific security. Sure, if there are very few participants, a small order might make a big influence on price and the penny stock because of its very small market cap could realize strong fluctuations in price. However that low trading volume that was responsible for big changes in price also results in very low liquidity. In this case, even though the trader against all odds managed to realize a large spike in price with a risky penny stock, he will not have the liquidity to close his position at that increased price. Trying to close the position in a low liquidity environment will only lead to the price going back down and the trader might find himself with a loss after trying to close their position, even though the stock rose in value significantly.

The next major area of importance is understanding the meaning of percentages in the declining of price. A stock that already went down 90% in one day might tempt a person to think that the worst is over and that it can only drop a maximum of 10% before it goes to zero. While that is true pertaining to the change in value of an asset while it is being owned, it is not true for the change in price one will experience if they buy after that 90% drop. If a stock for example drops 90% in value from 100$ to 10$, then it can only drop another 10$ which is the relevant consideration for someone who already owns the asset. However if that asset was bought after the 90% drop at 10$, it could drop another 90% the following day to 1$. In that case the person who bought at 10$ would experience a 90% loss. This can of course go on for as long as the minimum traded amount allows. It could drop again the following day with the same amount in percent resulting in a price of 0.1$ and so on. Understanding this will prevent unnecessary losses from mistakes in judgment.

*How to calculate risk*

The calculation is crucial and makes up such an important and unique part of the trading strategy that there is no perfect way. First one needs to decide how to apply the risk calculation, if it's on the portfo io as a whole, if one weighs the trades to a total maximum risk or if one hedges every trade individually. Calculating 1% risk of the full capital is straightforward. Just divide the amount of capital by the positions expected risk. For example, the stop loss is at 4%, meaning the trader expects a maximum of 4% and does not want to go over that, instead closing the position as soon as that 4% mark is crossed, whether with a stop loss order or manually. In this case to get the right position size one would simply calculate 5000$, the size of the account, divided by 4%, the risk of the position. The resulting 1,250$ are the position size to take, in which 1% of the account which is 50$ is risked if that positions drops 4% in price. In other words, 4% of 1,250$ are 1% of the account with 5000$.

For 1% risk:

$$Position\ size = \frac{Capital}{Risk\ of\ position}$$

Example:

$$Position\ size = \frac{5000\$}{4\%}$$

To get a larger or smaller percentage than 1%, one could take the right side of the equation and multiply it by 1.5 for 150% of the term meaning 1.5% risk. The other way by multiplying with a number smaller than one, for example dividing by two or multiplying by 0.5%.

For a risk tolerance per trade of 1.2%:

$$Position\ size = \left(\frac{Capital}{Risk\ of\ position}\right) \times 1.2$$

example:

$$Position\ size = \left(\frac{5000\$}{4\%}\right) \times 1.2$$

With this calculation the risk of the position is 60$ at 4% risk which is 1.2% of 5000$.

This is just a very trivial idea of how to make up your own calculation, not the perfect one, but a very basic idea of how percentage calculations work. This formula being simple and easy to use allows for calculation of basic risk related to expected losses based only on the stop level, however it does not factor in spreads, provisions of the broker and other factors that will drastically skew the risk away from the calculated level. I am just trying to give basic ideas on how to start forming your own calculations. For example to factor in provisions, one possible way that might work is to calculate position size based on the change in the dollar amount of risk due to provisions, since it is of predictable size and adds to the risk of the position.

One way to form an equation for this:

$$Position\ size = \left(\frac{100}{Risk\ of\ position}\right) \times (risk\ in\ \$ - Provision)$$

Instead of inserting the desired risk in % of the portfolio in this formula, it is directly inputted as the previously converted dollar amount in risk to allow for subtraction with the amount of provision that will factor in as additional risk, and position size is then calculated with that new value. if 1% risk of the portfolio are desired and the account size is 5000$ as with the previous example, then 1% of 5000$ are 50$, which would be the input for "risk in $". If the desired risk of the position was 1.2% of the account, then 1.2% of 5000$ are 60$. With that as input the formula would look like this:

1.2% risk to the account, broker charges 20$, stop loss at 4%, how big should the position be?

$$Position\ size = \left(\frac{100}{4\%}\right) \times (60\$ - 20\$)$$

The result in this case is 1000$, which means that when entering a position of this size and risking 4% of that position, then the total amount risked equals exactly the desired 1.2% of the account. The 4% that are risked in the position would result in a loss of 40$ and the provision added an additional 20$, so a total of 60$ where risked which is 1.2% of the account with 5000$.

In previous chapter I mentioned that the risk of a portfolio needs to be calculated and adjusted to promise consistent returns and reduced downside risk at any point in time. Ideally a trader should never risk more than 1% of their capital at any given time. Position sizing is one of the biggest if not the biggest reason that retail traders blow an account after only a few months. A great way to illustrate this is an experiment with a 50/50 coin flip. A person starts with a certain amount of capital and can bet a different amount every toss. Ideally the person does not lose all their capital and actually makes a profit. In an experiment the participants were told that there is a 60% chance of heads winning, and that the goal is to increase the capital they were given in the lowest number of tosses. It is obvious that over betting will wipe out all capital fairly quickly, for example when betting half of the capital in one toss, only two losses in a row will wipe out all capital. Two losses in a row are very likely as described in chapter one on clusters. When under betting, the capital should grow provided the participant only bets on heads but it will be very slow and unrealistic to be sustainable in a real life scenario. Despite the participants in this experiment often being finance students or professionals in finance they surprisingly made crucial errors that led to 28% of participants blowing up such as betting on tails even though they were told that there is a 60% chance of heads, over betting and betting erratically with seemingly no system. Even though everyone should have reached the goal of achieving a ten-fold increase of the given capital, only 21% achieved this. From this experiment we can learn that constant risk management is important as well as a good awareness of the risk/return ratio of trades. Additionally we see that gambling behavior occurs when there is no system or rules put in place and that this sort of behavior will certainly lead to a loss of money/ blowing the account. The optimal amount to bet each toss would have been 20% of the capital each round to allow for compounding. That means an increase of the bet after every win as the capital accumulates, and vice versa.

Since Position sizing is the possibly the biggest mistake retail traders can make and the fastest way to blow an account, it is crucial to determine the amount of risk for every position and adjust the money invested. If a person wanted to risk exactly one percent on any one position, it would take 100 losses in a row to blow up the account and lose all funds. For less than 1% for example risking .5% per position, it would be even harder.

When risking 1% for example on every trade, the risk is hedged but this system is still losing over time if the profits are not more than the risk or if the hit rate is under 50%. Because of that the risk-reward ratio is very important as well as avoiding mistakes that lead to a low hit-rate. The bigger the risk to reward ratio is, the faster the account will grow. A trading system that gets the position right 90% of the time sounds great, but even when risking less than 1% per trade this system can lose money if they lose more money in those 10% of the trades than they make in the other 90%. Most trading systems for sale by trading educators and scammers that sell signals take advantage of this fact and only advertise their hit rate and risk management but conveniently leave out the fact that the return is a negative value. Like with risk, the trader should have a limit for the risk-reward ratio before entering a trade. An example of a minimum value would be two, meaning that a trade will only be entered if the potential profits are twice the amount of the potential risk. Going with the previous example of risking 6% in a position and hedging position sizing to only expose 1% of risk on the whole account, the minimum amount of profit to be made would be 12% on the position or 2% of the whole account. Below that, if that was the minimum Risk-reward ratio required by the trader the position could not be entered and positions with these parameters would lead to reduced growth or even losses of capital. The risk reward ratio like the risk per position need to be carefully decided and calculated by the trader based on statistics and hit rate of previous trades to optimize growth. To sum up until this point, the trader needs to calculate the risk reward ratio and then the position size before entering a trade.

*Paper trading*

Before taking on the first trade a lot of sources will suggest to start paper trading first, meaning not investing actual money into a position but writing it down and keeping track of the money as if it were invested. On the positive side, this will show if a certain strategy or risk management is good in the long term and simulate more or less realistic returns that would have taken place if those positions were taken. Additionally, it might help eliminate fear of opening the first position and investing real money. Although I touched on this subject before in an earlier chapter, I need to get more in depth as this is a topic very relevant during the start of a trading career. The problem with paper trading that is often not mentioned is that a big part of being a successful trader is not being trained during paper trading: Control of emotions and discipline. It will be a lot easier to sleep at night when the positions don't have actual money invested and there is no risk of actual loss. The trader might find it very easy to stick to rules and discipline and may assume that it will be the same way when trading with real money. The step to trading with one's own money is actually a big step and will cause a big change in the persons trading- behavior.

A person who achieved very good returns on paper will likely not achieve the same returns when trading with real money and some traders might actually suffer a loss in capital instead, since once emotions play a part in trading and the untrained trader overestimated his abilities to stick with discipline, because of which he will start making mistakes such as breaking rules with position sizing or adding to loosing trades. A good step between paper trading and real trading would be to start slow. A misconception of starting slowly would be to invest less money, which actually increases risk because the trading costs and commissions will still be the same but the potential profit will be reduced. Also like in paper trading less emotional control is required so the trader might have an easier time sticking to discipline and avoid slipping into gambling behavior, but the profits will still be negligible if not nonexistent. A trader to make the step from paper trading has to invest his own money without hesitation and train himself to deal with the emotions associated with the risk. A good way to eliminate risk and make this transition easier is to start trading on longer time frames like the weekly candle chart instead of the 4h chart. Since the move that is being predicted takes place over a longer period of time, the trader will not be at risk of large profits or losses in a short period of time. When trading on a longer time frame, the stop and take profit lever are obviously further away from the opening level, so the same risk and potential profit are expected from the trade, but it takes more time such as weeks instead of only days, meaning that big changes in capital are very unlikely in a short period of time. The trader can step back more readily and reevaluate the position, decisions and his emotional state. Emotions and biases might be weaker in longer time frames but still present and therefore a good opportunity to be evaluated without too much risk. He can then gradually shorten the time frame, and if the hit rate does not go down and the average risk reward ratio of trades stays the same, then the trader will start achieving returns more quickly, although this then requires more emotional control, hedging and stricter discipline.

*Order types and their function*

The first order that comes to mind that is unfortunately also the most used by retail traders is the market order. When placing a market order the main priority of the transaction becomes getting filled at any price. A market order will have a direct influence of an assets price, because a large market order expresses a large demand for an asset. Since supply is the same, the price naturally rises. For this reason the order is completely avoided by institutional and private traders with large capital as they don't want to push up the price when buying an asset. Retail traders often feel a sense of urgency and experience a fear of missing out, then decide to buy or sell the asset at market price. This makes the entry level unclear and the position harder to hedge as every share might be executed at a different price far above the current market price. When placing a market order, a trader Is against very sophisticated high frequency algorithms that will certainly get the shares before you and sell them back to you at a higher price in a matter of nanoseconds. This sort of arbitrage will always take place when setting a market order, guaranteeing a less favorable price upon execution than the price that was indicated before placing the order.

A limit order on the other hand, specifies a price in which the trader wants to enter, usually below the current price for buying and above the current price for selling. The order is executed when a buyer is matched who wants exposure at that same level, which is usually when the price of the asset reflects that limit price. In times of high volatility the bid ask spread might deviate from the last price a lot more and the limit order could be filled that way as well. With a limit order, the shares when buying stock for example only get filled if the price meets the value that the trader set in their limit order. That way the trader guarantees that if they get filled, it is at the right level at which they wanted exposure to that asset, and every share is bought at the same price making it possible to calculate what the risk of that position exactly is.

*The stop loss order*

A stop order is a type of order placed at the beginning of a trade that triggers automatically without further input from the trader when the price moves below a certain price or in a short position moves above a certain level, therefore limiting the maximum losses of a trade to a certain predetermined level and guaranteeing transparence to the trader who can then calculate the risk of the position before entering it. The practicality of this order is controversial with everyone having a different opinion on it. It is very common among retail traders and almost always strongly emphasized by trading educators but their use in the institutional world of trading is debatable. What is obvious about the order is that the stop cannot be too "tight" as it is often called meaning not too close to the entry price of the trade, or else the trader risks having the trade automatically closed by the order through noise in the markets, and then moving in the speculated direction. If that is the case, then the trader now did not make any profit and actually made a loss, plus probably paid commission fees to the broker twice, even though the stock or other security actually moved in the direction that the trader was hoping for. As said before in a previous chapter, it is also often the case that the market will, apart from noise, move directly to the level where the stop is located at, and then in an often large move, go not only back to the entry level but further in the speculated direction. When a large amount of orders are at a certain level, in this case the stop level of the trader, then the market will often retrace to that level through the laws of supply and demand, and after hitting that level just resume its normal path. The reason for those large amount of stops all around the same level is that everyone is looking at the same chart. The trader does not have an edge by analyzing the price history of a stock or using indicators and different visual representations of price movement. Everyone has the same tools. The advantage of this is, that one can predict just like the institutional trader, where everyone else placed their stops and conclude that it might not be a good idea to do what everyone else does in this case. This way a retail trader might successfully emulate the success of the institutional trader. The implementing of a stop order should not be mistaken with simply deciding on a level where one will cut their losses and exit the position. It is very important to decide on a level to exit the trade at, to calculate the expected risk and adjust the position size accordingly. The discipline to stick to exactly that level is crucial too. But a level can be determined even though no stop order was placed. Instead it can be done manually. This carries the risk of the position moving far below the decided level before one notices and thus creates more unexpected losses than what was calculated. On the other hand it might drastically reduce the amount of trades where the trader gets "stopped out", meaning the stop loss order got triggered and the trade is over. By not placing a stop order but instead manually executing the closing of a trade, the trader ensures that the two scenarios which were just described cannot happen, in which the price just briefly moves to the exact stop order and then continues in the opposite direction back again. Using a stop loss order is up to the trader, but the risks and rewards should be clear. A wider stop loss on a larger time frame is not as prone to being falsely triggered as a stop order on a shorter trade where noise is more abundant. As you zoom out on a chart, the ups and downs often become less pronounced and a clear trend is more visible making a false triggering of a stop loss order obviously more unlikely. So the hit rate depends on the distance between entry price and stop price, but also on the time frame itself.

Remember that when hedging the size of a position to the total risk of the portfolio according to the total capital, it is not the amount risked in percent but the ratio of risk reward that matters. A wider stop does not mean more risk, but instead that a larger timeframe is used. The risk-reward ratio is what the risk should be derived from instead. For example a trade where 1% are risked and the desired exit level is at 2% profit, is a risk reward ratio of 2 and the exact same as a trade where 10% are risked and 20% profit are expected. The only difference is the time frame which is usually larger in the second example as volatility is limited. Ideally the risk per position never depends on the stop but instead is always hedged to the same value. This means that in a trade where the stop is at 10% loss, the trader will invest 10 times less, than with a trade where the stop is at 1%.

*Average true range*

The placement of a stop loss order or using the order at all can make or break a trade. It is imperative to decide on what to base the level for the stop, whether an actual stop loss order is used or not. What seems to be the most commonly used strategy, and the one that is being preached by the trading educators and brokers seems to be to keep the stop as tight as possible. The problems with this method are obvious as the trade now risks as explained before, to be stopped out by random noise, "stop hunting" and similar scenarios. They advocate for the stop to be just below the last resistance, the last point where the price moved to, and since they also recommend waiting for confirmation, the price will be slightly above that level where the stop is supposed to be placed according to them, and very likely to retrace back to that level. This severely influences the hit rate of the trading strategy and many trades will be unnecessarily lost.

One possibility is to base the stop on the average true range. It seems reasonable that the stronger the random movements of the market are, the larger the stop should be, to avoid getting the position closed. When calculating the stop based on the average true range, a wider range during higher volatility will increase the distance between entry level and the level where the stop loss is located, if the stop loss was based on a multiple of that average true range. For example, some traders base their stop placement so that it is twice as far from the entry level as the average true range is. using a method like this could have a positive effect on the amount of trades that get "stopped out", due to a too tight stop loss order that was placed. On the other hand, the risk reward ratio gets skewed, and the stop might be larger than it needs to. Additionally the average true range is only an indicator, and so called "lagging" because it uses information from the past and cannot predict the future. Past volatility is in no means an indication of future volatility and the average range might mean nothing in the next trading day. It is up to the trader to decide if it is useful more often than not, and depends entire on their calculations and trading strategy.

A typical trade might take place as followed: The trader for whatever reason after fundamental or technical analysis expresses interest in a security and believes that the price will rise. He decides on a level to cut losses and the minimum level to take profit. He evaluates if the risk to reward ratio is worth placing the trade and finally calculates the maximum position size. Note that this goes for a simple scenario like directly buying or selling shares of a security. Risk management and everything associated with entering a position will be greatly different when trading with derivatives or securities where leverage is used such as foreign exchange. When trading derivatives one needs to calculate the Greeks such as delta, decide on a strategy and what to hedge as well as the potential risk and profit that are not as obvious as with buying and selling stock.

*Overlooking percentage gain and misinterpreting profits*
An important fallacy to avoid, is looking at the actual cash amount that was gained or lost and not focusing enough on the percentage gain. In a winning trading system especially, it is very important to stay reasonable and have realistic expectations. Just because the very first week was very profitable, does not mean that this return is sustainable. The first week could, because of a number of

reasons or random events, be the most profitable week the trader had for years.

The risk is that the trader becomes greedy and changes his risk tolerance. He might believe that since the hit-rate has been consistently above 50% and most trades are winners, increasing the risk tolerance will yield faster and higher profits. When bargaining with risk tolerance due to greed, there is always the risk that the new position sizes start to become unreasonable and unsustainable. Losing streaks are inevitable and having a high risk allocation and entering a losing streak will create losses that outweigh the profits that were made. This can often lead to a downward spiral, where the trader falls into bad habits and starts to increase position sizes even more to compensate for losses, as they are sure that they will succeed in the long term based on their previous success.

Having too high expectations, either after experiencing a period of good profitability, or even at the start of the trading career can have a big negative impact on the quality of the portfolio and the traders emotions. One common cause of unrealistic expectations is looking at the cash amount instead of the percentage gain of the profits.

A new trader is very likely to make mistakes in position sizing and might feel that they are too small on their winning trades, and too big on their losing trades. This is completely normal and unavoidable but may lead to false expectations. It is obviously difficult to cope with a trade that went absolutely in the traders favor and rose by an unexpectedly high amount because of increased volatility, but barely made any tangible profit, due to position sizing.

Another reason for unsatisfactory profits might be that the portfolio is simply small and the trader attained unrealistic expectations from sources like trading educators who rarely talk about the percentage made on their portfolio but instead often talk about how much money they made on a given day in dollars directly. A return of 20% in a year is for a lot of people a very good return, especially since it outperformed the general market. It is enough for some to finance their life with. However in a small account, especially new ones that still did not experience the positive effects of compounding, those 20% might seem like a miniscule amount. The trader having seen the unrealistic figures given by trading educators for example or people with accounts ten times the size of theirs, will inevitably be disappointed with his own results, even though they might be very good.

The problem with having unrealistic and too high expectations as previously mentioned, is the risk of engaging in harmful gambling like behavior and ruining the profitability of the portfolio, but also a lack of confirmation that the system is working, since the trader believes that the profit is not enough and aims for more, when in reality it is impossible at this point in time which leads to them giving up.

*Misusing orders*

In a previous chapter I mentioned traders having very predictable and tight stop loss placements which often get triggered right before the market turns in their direction. These placed orders are then bought by institutional traders who then ironically get the liquidity they need for a big move. Instead of placing a stop directly underneath the previous resistance after a push in price, it might be better for the trader to wait for a pullback and base the entry on the same level where they would have placed their stop. In other words a trader can follow the successful institutional trader by entering a trade below the current price, at the level where the trader would have placed their stop. Additionally there is a misconception that with volatile securities the stop should be tighter to avoid higher risk. In reality a tight stop in a volatile market only guarantees that the hit rate of the trader goes down and he will be stopped out of the position very quickly. The stop needs to be at the appropriate level and the position sizing needs to be based on the size of the risk not vice-versa. Retail traders can make the mistake to invest erratically and try to invest the same amount into each trade, by basing their stop level on  the amount of risk they are willing to trade. After all, with a stop loss placed 2% under the current price, the trader can invest more money than with a stop loss placed 5% under the current price with the same amount of money risked. Because of bias the retail trader might convince himself that the tight stop is appropriate because he wants to invest more capital. In reality only the risk reward ratio matters. The stop needs to be where it needs to be. In a volatile market, a trader can look at the average true range to eliminate noise from the movements and follow a trend without having to close the trade because of noise in price. To sum up, the position size should always be based on the stop level, and the stop should be wider in a volatile market not tighter. A wider stop will mean a smaller position but since the market is more volatile the potential reward is also higher. Essentially the trader is hedging volatility since it does not matter if a security moves 10% or 5% in a day, the return over the long term will still be the same.

The previous examples and scenarios illustrate the importance of risk management very well. The potential risks of trading without proper risk management are a development of gambling behavior that leads to uncontrollable losses of capital, losing money even in a winning system with a hit rate of over 50% or making money for years only to be completely wiped out after the first financial crisis one experiences. Remember the previous chapter where I stated that when a stock falls 50%, it needs to gain 100% to reach the same level again. This ironically makes a financial crisis very favorable to the trader, because the recovery after a crisis is a lot more profitable than a normal uptrend. Sharp moves to the downside that are followed by more gradual and long term periods of rising prices can be very lucrative if properly taken advantage of.

# Conclusion

I am glad to have helped you, that you enjoyed this book and that it was in some or more ways useful.

I fully believe that with the right principles and attitude, anyone can have a successful career in trading and change a major part of their life for the better. Whether you start because you are aiming for an early or better retirement, for some extra money right now or even for a new career, the opportunity is massive and should be taken advantage of.

I sincerely wish every reader the best of luck in your future trading endeavors and an upstanding financial future.

I remember how my very first trade, a long time ago was an absolute winner. I bought stock in a medical company that rose by around 6% in only a couple of days. But since I had invested so little and did not factor in the broker fees, I barely made a profit. I learned a valuable lesson back then, along with other things that I learned from my later career and from other very experienced traders or hedge fund employees, that gave me the inspiration to write this book, and help others reach profitability and a positive career a bit quicker.

# Glossary

**compounding**
Interest adds to the interest already paid on the initial investment, causing exponential growth instead of linear growth of funds

**trader**
Person buying and selling in the financial markets

**blow up/ to blow an account**
To lose all the money, that was initially deposited into a trading account

**stop hunting**
A term given by traders to the alleged practice of institutional traders in which they enter a position at the same price, at which most retail traders do the opposite

**stop level**

The price at which the trader decided to close the trade to limit losses, with or without placing a stop-loss order

**take profit**

The Price at which the trader decided to close the trade to realize profits

**order**

A specific type of instruction to a broker mainly relating to buying and selling and setting specific prices for those actions

**portfolio**

The collection of all investments by a trader

**noise**

small fluctuations in price not relating to the general trend